Palace of poison

Sara Oliver

BookLeaf Publishing

India | USA | UK

Presentation by *BookLeaf Publishing*

Web: www.bookleafpub.com

E-mail: info@bookleafpub.com

ISBN : 9789357448536

First edition 2021

the tundra wolf

The Tundra wolf paces
'round a pebble in the snow
Arrows pierce the memories
Of a grail, we grieve to know

All it bore its fangs to
Forgotten in decay
Oh, red shadow
How it yearns to see another day

An eternal warmth from fur to frost
transcends beneath the storm
Shattered effigy humans
are fated to perform

Bones clamber to promise
And melt into the spring
Ethereal Galanthus
dashing up the ring

Rays melt evocation
Glowing 'round the clock
And when the pollen bleeds
You won't remember how to stop

chance

Dice tumble East
down a staircase built of mist
Spectral hands with blisters
bear the remnants of a kiss

A cufflink with initials
punctured to his wrists
The blood will sail West
to plant seeds in the abyss

Six dots stare North
over a precipice to hell
Tyche clasps him gently
and snaps open his shell

I unscrew all my bones
And build a nest out South
When blessed by a miracle
You must never ask how

vampire

Jam spread on a slice of moon
To devour within this tiny cocoon
A thirst,
Cursed for a vessel to burst
Penny-drop bites on a human tomb

snow kites

Calamity strikes when a fervent glacier
evolves to expand down the veins of nature
"You must regress to but an atom crafted by the
frost"
A colossal question lures soldiers
submitting to the shot

Humanity lies beneath a bed of bones
Built of treetops and polluted stones
"Crown me in the ground beneath the lily field
Where memories forget
they were meant to feel real"

The stained white petals in their naked stems
Poison soil with the corpses of snowmen
The destined ruler condemns you from beyond
the skies
Alluring us to use our veins and use its winds
To fly our kites.

sea breath

Amplified through the fog,
you cross as the ocean breathes,
discretely

Unseen by the blue lamps
that drift into rippled symphonies
and beg you to stay

An array of questions
circle your dreams
as the crimson waves decay

down your shins,
violently losing track
as the ocean
gently bleeds

genetic fame

A rich smile with an ocean of money
found a puddle on the street
She told him "I won't just give you honey,
I'll kidnap all the bees"
But after all the cameras had left her
and her Mother faded out,
She told him to bring back the ocean
so she could leave him in a drought

the sun lord

The Sun Lord worships night-lit women
with barcode teeth and hair like linen
He dresses love in silk attire,
through fire, the sky will cry all dark

His golden mask reflects her realms
A mind devoured by the Elms
Inside her moon, he coexists
For this,
the sun lord leaves in parts

in the mist

Celestial garden
Your poisons glazed
my heart with pure desire
A coat of gold
to callous the old,
tarnished palms of fire

Fortune whispered
down a drain of
shadows in the mist
A rotting ode
you left untold
when Love was just a wish

new beginnings

A curious fox
wanders past
a forest of closed doors
in choices, we find
a heart too blind
to love what's been ignored

A secluded bird
whistles downwards
a crevice in savage winds
in loss, we must choose
the unfortunate route
to remember how to begin

fireflies

In the cage of your palms,
A firefly
In the cage of your heart,
A noise
In soft lips, it beckons
a wild minded kiss
to tame what is yet to destroy

In the firefly's sprite,
A dreamy night
In the firefly's flight,
A wish
At midnight they gather
to feed the hearts
of memories that
cease to exist.

baboon

Blue baboon
sleeps on a high wire,
lips on the law of gravity

Stepless shoes
Death and diversity
falls for the tug of your salary

Red balloons
propelled by the strings
that beg for your penniless intimacy

Blue baboon
slips off the high wire
into our reckless society

writer's block

The vandal of my iris
wanders 'round a veiled prison
then unbuttons my mind
to find
the fingers of a corpse -

playing on melodic tusks
that yearn for words to give in
then strangling the alphabet
to find
a world unturned

desire

My blue heart ripples
For the warmth of dusk
Beneath the ocean's lid
is a world of love
I've never seen the clouds
So proud of their shadows
Against the ocean's lips
I dream of your touch

Purpose

How do you expect to manage the stupidity of
humility?
Faced by the rainforest eyes of mountain flies
Scavenging within you for a state of mind
Are you dreaming, lady of the nine nests?
Do you soak up the clouds in your quenched
breasts?
The ones with fire are the ones who conspire
to leave the old Queen in a puddle of debt
Would you finish the war in your arms of
distress?
Does the criminal ever confess to his jest?
Be or not be, you have broken the key
Now I am the lock sent to earth with no quest

I lie awake

Screaming trains
The fan panting for fresh air
Curtains choreographed by wind
Slithering down skin
A sun dressed up in moon
Living in my lungs
Sleeping wide awake,
inhaling me

star strings

Midnight blue embellished by her stolen
jewelled stars
He tramples on the construction of her shine,
Carrying her out of paradise
Time to time he looks into her eyes,
asks "why do wild stars shoot so fast
when they love?"
"Well, the crumbs of my past leave a trail for the
rats,
Marching and scratching, undoing my ghosts"
If only her knight let her flee to the coast
If only he kissed her once more
A torch with no force
Smothered in the blood of a silver cased corpse

Pink lemonade or Champagne?

A cerise coloured dress
and a pear coloured wagon
Pink lemonade or champagne?
Grizzlies with glasses
Nun's who smoke grass,
still using God's name in vain

A cerise coloured glove
A taupe coloured corset
Pink lemonade or champagne?
Sage for the spirits
A gun for a meal
The dragon tells her to be tame

A cerise coloured neck
and a rope made of silk
Pink lemonade or champagne?
A gregarious boy
with a chip on his tongue
and too many people to blame

A cerise coloured door

with indelicate bells
Pink lemonade and champagne?
A peevish sentence
with a rhetoric ring
Do not use God's name in vain

Love

A chest of scarlet butterflies
for my cityscape on a clear night sky
White pouring into a lunar glass
It feels like a line's finally been cast
My heart vessels gallop in the dusk,
my legs melt into buttercups
These goosebumps enslave my crimson skin
You're a craving but more...
you're a deep, deep shore
I pinch myself one and two and again
at rooster's wake to the hour of the pen
It's a blessing, a permanent dream
a beat
I make fire for men like you. I do.
I scavenge for wood while you turn blue
It's dangerous to love one like I love you
When you're not around,
my heart tugs
it pulls
since the lines on my palms were designed to
touch you
You're my gravity and I,
forever your pulse
Let our stems guide this forsaken love that we
own

and one day I may
let you sit on my throne
I wish you were here
in my arms,
through the tears,
over fears,
in my cusps,
then it would be just us
floating in love

www.ingramcontent.com/pod-product-compliance
Lightning Source LLC
Chambersburg PA
CBHW070737160726
48003CB00006BA/2557